John Paul Jones
A Photo Biography

by John Riley, M.Ed.

First Biographies
an Imprint of Morgan Reynolds, Inc.

Greensboro

John Paul Jones: A Photo Biography

Copyright © 2000 by John Riley

Allen County Public Library
900 Webster Street
PO Box 2270
Fort Wayne, IN 46801-2270

Photo credits: United States Naval Academy Museum

Library of Congress Cataloging-in-Publication Data

Riley, John, 1955-
    John Paul Jones : a photo-biography / by John Riley.-- 1st ed.
        p. cm.
    Includes bibliographical references (p.) and index.
    Summary: Describes the life and times of the well-known naval hero of the American
Revolution, John Paul Jones, who was called the father of the American navy.
    ISBN 1-883846-63-3 (library binding)
     1. Jones, John Paul, 1747-1792--Juvenile literature. 2. Admirals--United
States--Biography--Juvenile literature. 3. United States. Navy--Biography--Juvenile
literature. 4. United States--History--Revolution, 1775-1783--Naval operations--Juvenile
literature. [1. Jones, John Paul, 1747-1792. 2. Admirals. 3. United
States--History--Revolution, 1775-1783--Biography.] I. Title.

E207.J7 .R49 2000
973.3'5'092--dc21
[B]

                                                            99-089219

Printed in the United States of America

First Edition

Table of Contents

Boldface words are defined in **Words to Know**.

American Hero

John Paul Jones was a sailor. He helped the Americans fight the British in the **American Revolution**.

The British ships were more powerful. John wanted to prove that the Americans could beat the British.

John's ships won a big sea battle. The Americans were happy. Now they knew they could win against the British.

John Paul Jones was the "father of the American Navy."

John Paul Jones was a famous sailor.

Childhood

John Paul was born on July 6, 1747. He was born in **Scotland**.

John lived near the ocean. He swam and fished and floated toy boats on the water.

John liked to read and to add and subtract numbers. He knew this would make him a better sailor.

John wanted to go to sea. His parents found him a job on a ship. John packed his clothes and left home. He was 13 years old.

John found a job on a ship at age 13.

Young Sailor

John Paul sailed on a trader ship. The ship carried food, wood, and rum. It sailed from Scotland to the West Indies and on to America. One trip took a year.

John wanted to be captain of his own ship. He studied the stars and learned how to **navigate** a ship.

Being a sailor was hard work. But John loved it. He was happy at sea.

John wanted to be captain of his own ship.

with Six ——— Men, —— which are all Britains

Men, and no others ——— besides John Paul a Master

Man, Master for the present Voyage from Grenadoes and the West Indies

in America

One hundred and two Hogs heads Rum ——— William Kirkpatrick

One hogshead Ditto ——— John Grahame

One hogs head Ditto ——— Gilbert Patterson

One Tierce Ditto ——— William Donaldson

Eighteen hogsheads Ditto ——— Currie Buch and Co

Thirty four hogsheads Muscovedo Sugar ——— William Kirkpatrick Junr

Twenty Bales Cotton wool ——— George Campbell ———

Three Casks Ginger ——— William Kirkpatrick Junr

all British Sugar plantation product and brought directly

from thence

John Paul

I Do swear, That the Entry above written, now tendered and subscribed by me, is
a just Report of the Name of my Ship, its Burden, Built, Property, Number and
Country of Mariners, the present Master and Voyage: And that it doth further
contain a true Account of my Lading, with the particular Marks, Numbers, Quantity, Quality and Consignment, of all the Goods and Merchandises in my said Ship,
to the best of my Knowledge; and that I have not broke Bulk, or delivered any
Goods out of my said Ship since her loading in Grenadoes and the West Indies
no foreign Sails or such Cloth on board ——— So help me GOD.

Sworn before Us,
the first ——————— Day of Decemr 1770

Jas Lowrie Collector.

Jn Paul

Ship Captain

John changed ships. His new ship carried **slaves**. Slaves are people who are owned by someone else. Slaves do not get paid for their work.

John hated sailing on a slave ship. He quit and found another ship.

The captain on John's ship died. John became the new captain. He got the ship back safely.

John liked sailing to America. He wanted to live there.

John became a captain when he was 21 years old.

Trouble

John had a fight with a sailor. The sailor was killed. John ran away to America.

John changed his name to John Jones. He lived in Virginia.

The British demanded the Americans pay **taxes.** The Americans wanted to be independent.

The Americans and the British went to war in 1775. This war is called the American Revolution. John joined the small American Navy.

George Washington led the American colonies to war against the British.

War

John changed his name again. Now he was called John Paul Jones.

The new navy needed supplies. John captured a fort. He took all their supplies.

While sailing toward America John's ship was attacked. The battle raged for hours. Cannonballs slammed into the ship. Finally the British sailed away.

The American sailors cheered and sailed home.

John Paul Jones was an officer of the new American Navy.

New Ships

John sailed to France. Benjamin Franklin lived in France. He was an American.

Franklin got John a new ship. It was called the *Bonhomme Richard*. This was the French name for "Poor Richard." Poor Richard was the name of a book written by Benjamin Franklin.

John heard about 40 British ships heading to America. He hurried away from France. He wanted to catch the British ships before they reached America.

John met Benjamin Franklin in France.

"I Have Not Yet Begun to Fight!"

When John caught the British ships, one of them fired on the *Bonhomme Richard*. John's ship began to sink.

"Do you give up?" the British captain yelled across the water. The air was full of shells and bullets.

"I have not yet begun to fight!" John yelled back. The British ship sailed closer. There was time for one last shot.

Ka-boom! The British ship exploded. The British captain surrendered.

John sunk the British ship *Serapis* in a battle.

America's Finest Sailor

John moved to France. He looked for ships for the American Navy. In 1783 the Americans won the war.

John moved to Russia. He joined the Russian Navy. Then he returned to France. He died there on July 18, 1792.

John Paul Jones was one of America's first heroes. He helped to start the American Navy. Today you can visit his grave at the United States Naval Academy in Annapolis, Maryland.

John Paul Jones is buried in Maryland.

Timeline

1747—Born in Scotland on July 6.

1768—Becomes captain of his first ship.

1773—Moves to America.

1775—Joins the American navy.

1778—Defeats a fleet of British ships.

1779—The *Bonhomme Richard* defeats the British ship *Serapis*.

1780—Moves to France.

1790—Joins the Russian navy.

1792—Dies in Paris, France.

Words to Know

American Revolution: [ah-MER-uh-kan reh-vah-LOO-shun] the war the American colonies fought for independence from Great Britain.

navigate: [NAV-uh-gate] to sail a ship.

Scotland: [SCOTT-lund] one of the countries of Great Britain.

slaves: [SLAYVS] a person who is owned by another person.

taxes: [TACKS-is] fees charged by a government to its people.

Further Reading

Morrison, Samuel Eliot. *John Paul Jones: A Sailor's Biography*. Little Brown & Co. Boston, 1959.

Simmons, Clara Ann. *John Paul Jones*. Naval Institute Press. Annapolis, MD, 1997.

Syne, Ronald. *Captain John Paul Jones*. William Morrow & Co. New York, 1968.

Walsh, John Evangelist. *Night on Fire*. McGraw-Hill Book Company. New York, 1978.

Websites

John Paul Jones House—Photo Tour:
http://www.seacoastnh.com/touring/jpjcollect.html

A Revolutionary Webquest:
http://library.thinkquest.org/11683/JPJones.html

Places to Write

United States Naval Academy Museum
118 Maryland Avenue
Annapolis, MD 21402
(410) 293-2108

Index